PRAISE FOR

The ADHD Sibling Challenge

How to Thrive When Your Brother or Sister Has ADHD
An Interactive Family Guide

"Brilliant! Unique! Based on decades of seeing patients, Dr. Herskovitz has put together a concise, user-friendly, reliable, and practical manual that parents can use with their children. This hugely needed book fills a tremendous gap, and it comes from one of the smartest, gentlest, wisest clinicians in the field."

—Edward Hallowell, M.D., co-author of *Driven to Distraction* and *Delivered from Distraction*

"*The ADHD Sibling Challenge* addresses a neglected but important topic for any family with an ADHD child. Living with a sibling with ADHD can be challenging and this interactive book will help kids and their families better understand and manage their daily lives in a creative and positive way. A much-needed addition to the ADHD literature."

—Daniel A. Geller, M.D., Michele and David Mittelman Family Chair in Child and Adolescent Psychiatry, Massachusetts General Hospital, Associate Professor of Psychiatry, Harvard Medical School

"Dr. Bart Herskovitz has written an excellent book for families facing the challenge of an ADHD child. His recognition of the struggles of siblings amidst the chaos of ADHD behavior fills a gap in our field and is a unique contribution. The Workbook format creatively engages parents and kids in a process of greater understanding and opens them to a path of emotional healing. I look forward to recommending this wonderful book to families in need."

—Arthur G. Mones, Ph.D., Clinical Professor, Derner Institute for Psychological Studies, Adelphi University, Certified IFS Therapist and author, *Transforming Troubled Children, Teens, and Their Families: An Internal Family Systems Model for Healing.*

"This book and its exercises should be a major boost to families managing ADHD. It offers recognition and clarity to siblings, who often live in the midst of conflict and uncertainty."

—John J. Ratey, MD, Clinical Associate Professor of Psychiatry, Harvard Medical School, co-author of *Driven to Distraction* and *Spark: The Revolutionary New Science of Exercise and the Brain*

"Children who have been given the diagnosis ADHD struggle to control their impulsive parts and, consequently, can be challenging for their siblings to live with and take up a lot of their parents' attention. As a result, siblings often suffer but don't express their feelings for fear of adding to their parents' burden. This book is written for them. Its clarity and format of simple but revealing exercises helps parents become more aware of the siblings' dilemmas and serves as a guide for parent-sibling discussions that will ease tensions and lead to important changes. Highly recommended!"

—Richard Schwartz, Ph.D., Developer of the Internal Family Systems model of psychotherapy, Adjunct faculty, Harvard Medical School

"In the field of ADHD much attention, especially among professionals, has focused on children with ADHD and their parents. Unfortunately, the siblings of kids with ADHD are often a forgotten population. Dr. Bart Herskovitz, a well-known psychiatrist who has specialized for more than 30 years in working with youngsters with ADHD and their families, has written a wonderful book especially geared for the siblings of children with ADHD. With much empathy and understanding he describes the behaviors associated with ADHD and the special problems faced by siblings. He offers practical and realistic strategies together with exercises for siblings to help them cope and thrive in a family in which a child has ADHD. Dr. Herskovitz has provided siblings, parents, and professionals alike with an impressive resource that I highly recommend."

—Robert Brooks, Ph.D., Faculty, Harvard Medical School (part-time), co-author, *Raising Resilient Children; Raising a Self-Disciplined Child*

the ADHD sibling challenge

HOW TO THRIVE WHEN YOUR BROTHER OR SISTER HAS ADHD
AN INTERACTIVE FAMILY GUIDE

BARTON S. HERSKOVITZ, MD

ILLUSTRATED BY SARAH LYNNE REUL

Great Island Press | Needham • Massachusetts

The ADHD Sibling Challenge
How to Thrive When Your Brother or Sister Has ADHD
An Interactive Family Guide

Barton S. Herskovitz, MD
www.ADHDSiblingChallenge.com

Great Island Press
Needham • Massachusetts

Cover and interior design by Dunn+Associates, www.Dunn-Design.com

Publisher's Cataloging-in-Publication Data
Names: Herskovitz, Barton S., author.
Title: The ADHD sibling challenge : how to thrive when your brother
or sister has ADHD, an interactive family guide / Barton S. Herskovitz, MD.
Description: Includes bibliographical references. | Needham, MA: Great Island Press, 2020.
Identifiers: LCCN 2019903954 | ISBN 978-1-7338328-3-0 (pbk.) | 978-1-7338328-4-7 (ebook)
Subjects: LCSH Attention-deficit hyperactivity disorder—Family relationships.
Attention-deficit hyperactivity disorder—Popular works.
Attention-deficit disorder in adolescence—Problems, exercises, etc. | Brothers and sisters.
Children with disabilities—Family relationships.
BISAC FAMILY RELATIONSHIPS / Attention Deficit Disorder (ADD-ADHD)
FAMILY RELATIONSHIPS / Siblings
JUVENILE NONFICTION / Family / Siblings
Classification: LCC RJ506.H9 .H472 2020 | DDC 618.92/8589—dc23

contents

This book is dedicated to every child who has a sibling to share life's joys and frustrations. My hope is that it will increase communication and compassion between siblings, as well as with their parents.

introduction

In my work as a child psychiatrist, when a family comes to me with a child who is diagnosed with ADHD, I spend most of my time and energy helping that child *and* the parents. The child may need therapy or perhaps medication. The parents usually need help with parenting strategies.

The family members who are most often left out of the therapeutic process, however, are the siblings of the child with ADHD. These brothers and sisters have to coexist with a sibling who may have great difficulty with skills like sharing, waiting one's turn, acting in a sensitive and calm manner, and cooperating with the family schedule.

This book was specifically written in recognition of the significant challenges faced by these non-ADHD siblings. It will help these youth understand their own circumstances as well as those of their siblings who have ADHD. It will support them in learning to apply strategies for asserting their own needs. Parents, too, will acquire a richer understanding of the challenges faced by these siblings and will be better able to provide guidance and support to meet these challenges.

Aimed at the siblings and parents, it will hopefully provide an important step in creating more balance and mutual understanding in your family.

—Barton S. Herskovitz, MD

OVERVIEW **for parents**

Please take the time to carefully read all of Part I before you introduce this book to your child. This part provides an overview of important challenges that may be present in your family. Hopefully, the insights in Part I will better enable you to support your children in understanding and coping with their siblings' ADHD.

In Part I you will learn about:

- Family dynamics unique to living with and raising children diagnosed with ADHD

- Research about non-ADHD siblings

- Strategies to support children with and without ADHD

When you move on to Parts II, III, & IV with your child, please be prepared to guide them through the stories and activities, especially if children are younger than thirteen years old. The content and your child's responses may raise a variety of issues about your family. You can discuss them with your child as you read them together—or return to them later. Sometimes children may not be willing to discuss family issues with you. That's fine, as well. They may become more open over time.

In Parts II, III, & IV you will find:

- A brief description of ADHD

- An overview to help siblings understand the purpose of this book

- Checklists and surveys to help you focus on important family issues from your child's point of view

- Engaging stories and activities to help children identify and talk about their experiences and feelings related to their siblings

- Helpful hints for using the strategies learned throughout the book

- Help for non-ADHD siblings to not become too hard on themselves, and to employ better self-care

In the appendices you will find:

- A short chapter about medication, if you feel that applies to your family situation

- Review and Summary Pages you might find helpful to refer to with your child

- A list of ADHD resources for parents

publisher's note and disclaimer

This publication attempts to provide accurate and authoritative information about the conditions and scenarios that are discussed. It intends to provide information for the reader to evaluate with due diligence. It is not intended to render psychiatric, psychological, or professional services and should not be considered professional advice.

If expert medical advice, guidance, consultation, or counseling is needed, do seek the services of a competent professional.

A Note on Language

English has no good pronouns that mean "his or her" or "he or she." Rather than repeat these awkward phrases throughout the entire book, the popular convention of using "they," "them," and "their" to represent both singular and plural, male and female pronouns is employed. This has some limitations, but it's a neutral solution that keeps the manuscript flowing.

For Readers of the eBook Edition and Library Borrowers

Many exercises in this book ask you to circle, mark or write things. Since you can't do this on many ebook readers, and you're not allowed to do it on the library's copy, please download our PDF from which you can print out all of the "activity pages" in this book, as well as Appendix II.

You can find the PDF at *www.ADHDSiblingChallenge.com/resources*.

PART ONE: **for parents**

You've already taken a wonderful step just by securing this book to use with your family. You'll learn more about what your children with and without ADHD think, feel, and need, to make changes that will help the whole family.

Using the valuable process of actively listening to your children you will gain information that can be used to direct next steps for increased family harmony and unity.

Parenting a Child with ADHD

Parenting is a challenging job. If you're reading this book, you have at least one child with significant self-control or compliance challenges. Raising this child is an enormous task. Books, support groups, and professionals (in schools or in the private sector) can help you. In addition, an ongoing commitment to learning about and meeting the needs of your other children, especially as they relate to ADHD issues in your household, is crucial to the family's wellbeing.

Balancing Diverse Needs

Parenting your child diagnosed with ADHD is an ongoing process that takes practice. A key way to ensure all of your children enjoy success is to support their needs as individuals. This includes children with and without ADHD. Teaching children to be fair to others, to be considerate and respectful, and to follow through

on completing tasks allows every child to feel competent and validated. For the child with ADHD this is especially important and must be a priority.

Understanding and meeting the needs of your other children more fully will make them happier and less likely to provoke or ostracize the child with ADHD. Often, in trying to "help" the situation, siblings with brothers or sisters with ADHD act overbearing, judgmental, aggressive, or passive-aggressive. Unfortunately, those behaviors make your household feel less safe and predictable for everyone. Remember, even kids who manage well still need your ear, your empathy, your acknowledgment, and special time alone with you.

In addition, many siblings of children diagnosed with ADHD often have some ADHD symptoms themselves. Most often, however, one child exhibits challenging behaviors more frequently and with greater intensity, which leads to family disruption. The fact that you may actually have multiple children dealing with symptoms of ADHD, makes this book especially useful to your family.

A. Family Dynamics and ADHD

The presence of ADHD creates unique interpersonal family dynamics. Because children with ADHD have a hard time stopping certain behaviors, repetitive actions can take on a coercive quality, e.g., badgering, yelling, interrupting, poking. Families can easily begin a cycle of reciprocal coercive behaviors when others respond in controlling ways. For instance, parents can easily begin to nag more, yell more, and make frequent threats about consequences. Siblings may also yell, push back, and resort to harsh words.

Another troublesome dynamic can develop around one child becoming stuck in a negative role in the family, such as "troublemaker" or "liar." Siblings of children with ADHD can then take on the characteristics of an opposite role, "the good child" who may sometimes subtly put down their sibling who has ADHD or become overly invested in being a child who has no problems.

Finally, too often, the needs of the child with ADHD become dominant, and it becomes hard to carve out the time and energy to address your non-ADHD children's needs—as well as your own needs. These unfortunate patterns and others result in increased emotional tension in the family.

Such dynamics and others like it will be brought into focus throughout this book. Ideas and strategies to shift family patterns to ones that are less rigid and provide more options for children to express their needs and facilitate family cohesion will be presented.

Moving Forward through Acceptance and Understanding

The siblings of children with ADHD experience the same range of feelings that you or their challenging sister or brother feel. These feelings may include:

- Confusion about the "rules of the road" in the household

- Frustrations about issues related to "fairness"

- Sadness based on family struggles

- Guilt for being a "normal" or "typical" child or for being a "problem" child

- Anxiety about their place and importance within the family

Encouraging family members to express and accept these and other feelings teaches them to handle feelings in healthy ways. For children, particularly those with siblings who have ADHD, these skills allow their emotional development to proceed with little disruption.

B. Research about Non-ADHD Siblings

Judy Kendall, RN, PhD, published a paper in 1999 that reinforces my own observations and work of the last four decades.

Disruption of Family Life

Disruption of family life was the most frequent problem mentioned by siblings. Disruptive behaviors identified by siblings included aggression (physical, verbal, self-destructive, or passive-aggressive), emotional and social immaturity, out-of-control hyperactivity, academic underachievement and learning problems, family conflicts, poor peer relationships, and difficult relationships with extended family.

One type of disruption involves the child with ADHD doing something that needs attention or affects others, such as badgering, interrupting, dawdling, and so on. Family members' responses to these behaviors cause additional disruptions. For example, brothers and sisters might mimic disruptive behaviors, siblings could take revenge or escalate the disruptive event, or family communication patterns, such as yelling, fighting, avoiding, denying, or excusing may increase the chaos.

Effects of Disruption

From Kendall's study, we also learn that many siblings feel victimized by their ADHD sibling, especially when facing physical violence, verbal aggression, manipulation and control. They feel deprived because their privacy is often intruded on, so they need to be constantly "on guard." Studies show that many siblings feel that their parents often minimize or disbelieve the seriousness of the aggression. Children may also feel angry and resentful at the perceived lack of appropriate parental response to their concerns. Often, when these children retaliate against their ADHD siblings, they will be overly aggressive because of this underlying anger at the parents. Older siblings often feel that parents are inept at raising a younger ADHD child and can tend to be judgmental and harsh when trying to advise a younger sibling.

Some siblings have mixed feelings about their need to take care of and protect their brother or sister with ADHD. Some siblings feel important and competent when helping out with an ADHD child. Most siblings, however, are ambivalent. They may feel parents expect them to play with or help their sibling with ADHD. Yet, too often, during these activities siblings become targets of that child's aggression. Parents consider typical siblings responsible enough to help out, but discourage them from complaining. These youths are left with little power, and may receive minimal recognition for their work.

A major concern for parents to consider is that siblings who become more resigned to their situation can *develop an image of themselves as unworthy of love, attention, care, or protection*—thus leading to lowered self-esteem.

Sorrow and Loss

Another finding that can be difficult for parents to acknowledge is that siblings of ADHD kids endure high levels of sorrow and loss. The most obvious level of loss is the amount of parental time and attention that must be focused on the ADHD child, thus limiting the parents' availability for other family members.

The effects of disruption and victimization often cause feelings of loss. For instance, many vacations can be ruined; mornings and bedtimes are often fraught with tension—and additional tension is created when parents fight about how to handle the ADHD child. Siblings often feel embarrassed by the actions of their ADHD family member. And siblings often worry about their sibling's future.

Loss and sorrow can also occur when siblings feel an expectation to be invisible; they perceive that the parents don't offer enough parental help or attention. Some children suppress their own needs and become more vulnerable to anxiety or depression.

C. How to Help Your Non-ADHD Children

For children the presence, patience, and affection of parents are the keys to building trusting and meaningful relationships. In addition, the approaches described below are offered to create simple changes parents can use to greatly improve communication between themselves and their children. These approaches provide the type of positive attention children need to thrive. These include:

- Active listening

- Providing appropriate praise

- Setting aside special one-on-one time

- Engaging your child in shaping the family's dynamics.

Using these approaches, as you engage in the workbook activities found in sections II, III, and IV, helps your children:

- Identify and accept feelings they are experiencing

- Begin to feel more engaged in improving the family team.

Active Listening

Active listening is a valuable technique to encourage sharing and communication. Ask your non-ADHD child how they feel about a situation and listen to their answer. Ask questions *only* to clarify or gather more detail. Wait a few moments before you add your own thoughts. You want your child to reveal as much as possible about their feelings, thoughts, and ideas so that you will know better what they need from you.

Here are two examples:

Example 1.

Parent: Bobby – you seem upset. Do you want to tell me what's bothering you?

Bobby: I'm sick of Sammy taking my things. You never do anything about it!

Parent: I know it's hard when he keeps breaking our rules. What has he taken?

Bobby: He took my trading cards again. He'll lose them. It's just totally unfair!

Parent: I know it is. It isn't fair for him or any of us that he has trouble with self-control. You sound frustrated with Dad and me because we can't get him to behave.

Bobby: Yeah! Exactly! I think you guys are just too easy on him.

Parent: Sounds like you think we should act differently towards him. Do you have any ideas that you think would work better?

Notice that first the parent acknowledges the child's feelings, and then asks for more details about what they feel or think.

In this example, the parent acknowledges how hard things are for everyone, including the ADHD child, but does not make excuses or defend.

Example 2.

Anna: I'm so sick of Brianna's tantrums!! I hate her!! I hate this family!!

Parent: Wow, Anna you sound so upset!

Anna: Who wouldn't be upset! Every day Brianna argues with you, and you argue with her. It's too upsetting to live here!

Parent: Yes, Anna, I see what you mean. You're right, there is probably too much arguing by everyone. I'm not happy when I engage with Brianna either.

Anna: So, why don't you find a better way to deal with her?

Parent: Actually, we're meeting with someone soon to help us with that. I'm sure it's been very hard for you to watch all the struggles in our house. We don't want you to live somewhere else, but we understand that you want a break from the tension.

Anna: I just hate my sister!

Parent: Well, what else is bothering you about Brianna?

Anna: She just never does what you ask her to do. Then you end up either nagging her or threatening her, and then she ends up in a tantrum.

Parent: Sounds like it 's just so hard for you when she resists dad or me. You must be so sick of our struggling with her.

Anna: Exactly! Who would want to listen to that every day? Plus, then you have no energy left for me. I probably hate that the most.

Parent: So, actually you're feeling neglected as well as being upset that dad and I get into struggles with Brianna.

Anna: Yes, I guess so.

Note again that the parent inquires for more information and more examples, but does not become defensive. The parent validates what the child is feeling, as painful as it is to hear.

Praise

It is important to find additional ways to praise siblings for their efforts to care for or help their ADHD sibling. Identifying and recognizing their efforts is critical. For instance, when your non-ADHD child helps out in a positive way, try giving them a quick hug—and say "thanks for being so patient," or "thanks for helping your brother right then." Even brief, small signs of appreciation will provide important validation for a child who may feel quite burdened, and sometimes invisible, as we will discover.

If your child shows signs of perfectionism or excessive self-blame, it is important to help them learn to take risks. Praise them for being "imperfect" and for being more spontaneous. Help them learn to laugh at themselves. Humor is very important in helping fend off the dangers of taking oneself too seriously. Help everyone see that there are no "right" answers in any situation involving ADHD. No expert, no parent, always knows the perfect response. It's trial and error. Essential to the process is the need to decrease the overt conflict and struggle in the house.

To help keep things lighter and more positive, get yourself the care or counseling you need. You'll have more to give to yourself, your partner and all your children.

Special One-on-One Time

If your child is most worried about receiving less attention, set aside special times to give them your undivided attention and share activities with you alone (beyond the exercises in this book). These times should be regular, substantial, and include interactions with you. This special time solidifies the child's sense of being truly important. Arranging for some respite for the family is also helpful. If the ADHD child can go away (to summer camp, for instance), you've created a wonderful opportunity for other family members to bond in different ways. Using babysitters or mother's helpers more extensively, even while you're at home in the after-school and early-evening hours, can help tremendously by providing nurturing and support to the family system, as well as provide needed breaks for parents.

Family Dynamics

If your child is most concerned that rules are unevenly enforced, explain that each child may have different consequences for disobeying rules, depending on their ability to learn from specific consequences. Although you, as a parent, will do your best to be fair, fair doesn't always mean equal.

Make plenty of room for siblings to complain or express their confusion about how rules are enforced and consequences applied. If your child feels that the ADHD child is "lucky" to get away with certain lighter consequences, ask, "Would you truly rather be the one who has ADHD?"

Siblings must deal constantly with their ADHD brothers or sisters. Do involve them constructively in formal discussions about their feelings and their active roles in family patterns; this can help them feel empowered. Feeling more valued and acknowledged will go a long way to helping them tolerate their feelings of loss. It will also help them feel worthwhile, powerful, and lovable.

Of course, if significant concerns emerge from your discussions, consult a counselor or therapist who is familiar with ADHD to help you ensure that all of your children's needs are being addressed.

Further Guidelines before Reading This Workbook with Your Child

1. It may be hard for your child to talk about certain issues. Some of the questions will invite your child to reveal a good bit about their feelings and thoughts. Some children may not be comfortable with this level of self-revelation. Never force a child to talk about something they are not ready to discuss.

    If the checklist questions in Part II seem too personal for your child, then just move on to the next section, "Think about Your Family: The Hard Times," which asks less of the child. You can revisit the checklist later, if desired, once your child feels safer exploring this material.

    The checklist provides ideas about how your child feels now about the family and their sibling. Use these insights to determine what issues should be addressed in more depth as your child and you complete the workbook together.

2. One useful strategy is for you to model the ability to comment on your own thoughts and feelings. An example might be, "I notice that I have mixed feelings about things that happen in our family. Part of me feels angry about misbehavior, and another part realizes that I should have given you kids advance notice about when we needed to leave the party."

3. This workbook is aimed at helping siblings cope and thrive. If the sibling often seems sad or angry or shows other persistent, troubling emotions or behavior, you should strongly consider having that child evaluated by a competent mental health professional. Of course, the same is true for your ADHD child. Counseling is often a necessary and useful part of a comprehensive treatment plan for ADHD.

4. Take time alone with your child to work on the activities in this book, separate from other special times together. If this displaces all other shared activities, your child may resent and resist further workbook exercises.

5. As you listen to your child share perceptions about the family, you may learn things that make you want to change some of your parenting choices. Counseling or education for yourself will help you develop alternative parenting strategies.

6. How to motivate your child to read and work on this activity book.

This book can be quite engaging, but parts of it require a good bit of work, reflection, and patience. The results of reading the book and doing the activities will be very gratifying. The intent is for you and your child to read this book together, so that your child can talk to you about their feelings, ideas and reactions to living with a sibling with ADHD. A major goal is for your child to have your ear and your attention, as they think and talk about their life in your family.

Some older kids will want to read it on their own. This is fine, especially if they are willing to subsequently go over their reactions and some of the activities with you.

Many kids will need some additional motivation to work on this book. One motivator is having a special time with you to work on it. Other incentives can be very useful, too.

Here are some ideas:

A. Set up a schedule for your child to work on it with you for about 30 minutes per week. At the end of 30 minutes, make some hot chocolate or popcorn together.

B. If your child can work longer, eg, an hour, or can work on 3 different occasions, reward them with an outing to Starbucks, or to an ice cream shop.

C. Try using electronics to motivate or reward your teen.

D. Using money as a reward can be okay, too. Consider it wages for work performed for the good of the family.

Be inventive, and don't worry if your strategy feels like bribery. That's a common strategy used to encourage kids to do numerous things that are good for them.

PART TWO: for kids and parents
thinking about your family

activity 1
An Explanation of ADHD for Children and Parents

Begin working either alone or with your parent by visiting some basic information about ADHD. Try reading the next few lines out loud.

ADHD means

A Attention

D Deficit

H Hyperactivity

D Disorder (medical condition)

These words may sound strange. What do they mean?

ADHD is a medical condition that lessens a person's ability to pay attention and control their actions. All kids sometimes have trouble paying attention, or following directions, or keeping track of their belongings, or sitting still. But kids with ADHD, whose brains are a little different from most people, have trouble with those things more of the time.

It's important to know a couple of things. First, if your sibling has ADHD, it's not anyone's fault. Your sibling may not always act like others, but everyone, with the help of parents, teachers and other important people in their lives, can improve their behavior and be successful.

Second, it's important for you to know that lots of kids either outgrow ADHD or, as time goes by, learn to behave more maturely.

As you read this book, you'll come across many examples of behaviors that occur with ADHD and helpful things you can do to respond.

activity 2
An Overview for Siblings

Your mom or dad found this book for you to help make your family life better.

However, you may not be too interested in reading this book or doing the activities. You may feel that you already have too much to deal with, living with a brother or sister who has ADHD. But this book will be worth it! You will learn better ways to get YOUR needs met, as well as better ways to deal with your brother or sister when they are being difficult. You will get to know your feelings better, and it will feel good to have this knowledge.

You will hopefully get some special attention from your parent, who will either read this book with you, or talk with you about it. Just work on it for 15 minutes to a half hour at a time.

You also may know someone else who has ADHD, besides your sibling. It's important to know that ADHD can take different forms. It can look different in different people.

Anyway, you live with a brother or sister who has attention deficit hyperactivity disorder (ADHD). That means that something is different and special about how their brain works.

Kids who have ADHD are wonderful in many ways: sometimes, they might have lots of energy, think up great ideas, and be very fun to play with.

But at other times, they may be hard to be around. They might have trouble sitting still, being quiet, being nice or considerate, being on time, and getting homework done.

They often try things that you wouldn't expect. Sometimes that's fun, but sometimes it can be a little scary, too.

They also may have trouble getting going in the morning.

They may run late because they can't find their things or because they want to do one last thing before leaving the house.

Many families struggle a lot when a child has ADHD. You might hear a lot of yelling, arguing, teasing, frustration, and confusion.

(Remember, for the sibling who has ADHD, this can mean that they know they are causing problems, even when they don't mean to—and are even trying their best to cooperate. In this book, we will hope to help you understand more about what life is like for your sibling who has ADHD. One has to imagine that it's often not fun to be the kid who has ADHD.)

As you go through the book with your parent, you'll discover stories to read, activities to try, and important things to talk about with your mom or dad. You'll get to share your thoughts and feelings while your mom or dad listens to you.

Remember—there are no right or wrong answers. It's just important to be as honest about your feelings and thoughts as possible.

Reading this book will help you understand your family better. The activities will help you and your family come up with some new ideas about how to live more happily.

activity 3
The Good Times

We'll talk later about challenges in your family. Right now, take time to think about and remember some great moments. Let's find out about what you enjoy most about your brother or sister.

Choose to do either A or B:

A. Write about some of the things that you like and enjoy about your brother or sister who has ADHD.

_____

_____

_____

_____

OR

B. Circle the words and phrases that describe your brother or sister:

Funny	Lively	Full of energy	Loving
Creative — lots of ideas	Very easy going	Caring	Honest
Fun to talk with	Interested in things	Fun to play with	Generous
Spontaneous — does things that are surprising			

Next, using the lines below, write down what actions do you take **toward your sibling** that make you either proud or happy? Examples of this may be playing together or helping with homework, finding misplaced objects or including your sibling when you have friends over to play.

_____

_____

activity 4
Checklist

Note for parents:

Your child's responses to the checklist below will provide indications about how your child feels now about the family and their sibling. I will be inviting your child to be a "detective", to become curious about their reactions to different statements and scenarios about the family and about their sibling. Hopefully, you will hear their concerns and observations about such issues as fairness, how people treat each other, feelings of burden, worry, and sadness. You can take note of their responses to help you in all of your discussions surrounding this book.

In terms of timing, you can discuss some of them with your child now (by asking for examples or asking more about their feelings about situations described), or return to them later as you read this book together.

Either way, use these insights to determine which issues should be addressed in more depth as you work on the book together.

Sometimes, children may not be willing to discuss family issues with you. That's fine, as well. They may become more open over time. If the checklist questions below seem too personal for your child, then just move on to the next section, "Think about Your Family: The Hard Times," which asks less of the child. You can revisit the checklist later, if desired, once your child feels safer exploring this material.

Let's Get Started!

Family life involves various people and activities, and sometimes it's hard to keep everything straight! Now you have a chance to think about your family and the things that happen in your household. You and your parent can be "detectives" to uncover how you feel and what you think about some of the things that go on in your family. Again, there are no right answers. These questions are just to get you thinking about life in your family.

   Look at this checklist. When you see the word sibling here, it generally refers to your brother(s) or sister(s) with ADHD.

   • Read each statement and decide how you feel about it. Do you agree, feel unsure, or disagree?

   • Check the box that best shows your answer.

Issues in Your Household	Often	Sometimes	Almost Never
My sibling is more easy-going than I am.			
My parents agree on how to handle my sibling.			
I try to be understanding of my sibling.			
My sibling embarrasses me around other kids.			
My sibling is funny and a lot of fun.			
Punishments in my family seem fair.			
I try to get my sibling into trouble.			
I have to be well-behaved so my parents won't be so stressed.			
I feel sad that my sibling has ADHD.			
I worry that family activities or trips will be disrupted by my sibling.			
My parents let my sibling get away with too much.			
My sibling leaves my belongings alone.			
I worry about my sibling with ADHD.			
I correct my sibling more than I should.			
My sibling is mean to me.			
My sibling tries hard to cooperate.			
I have to be perfect. I feel like I shouldn't have any problems.			

activity 5
The Hard Times

Think about the way you and your parents act when your sibling misbehaves or gets in trouble. Think about a common struggle that occurs when your sibling with ADHD misbehaves or does not cooperate.

Write down a brief description of the struggle here:

_____

1. On a scale of 1 to 5, circle the number that shows how **you** might feel or react when you're with your sibling at those times.

Patient		**Neutral**		**Annoyed**
1	2	3	4	5

Caring		**Neutral**		**Mean**
1	2	3	4	5

Calm		**Neutral**		**Upset/Yelling**
1	2	3	4	5

2. Think about your parents.

How does your **mom or dad usually react to your brother or sister** in the same situation? Circle the number that shows it.

Calm		**Neutral**		**Upset/Yelling**
1	2	3	4	5

3. Now do at least one of the following three activities.

A. Answer these questions.

A feeling I often have about my ADHD sibling is…

_____

_____

What actions do you take **toward your sibling** that make you unhappy with yourself or sad?

_____

_____

_____

_____

_____

If I could make a wish, what would I most want to be different in our lives?

_____

_____

_____

_____

OR

B. Draw a picture that shows how you sometimes feel about your sibling.

OR

C. Keep A Diary. A diary is a written record of what happens in your life. Talk with your parent about getting a reward if you write in your diary for at least three days in one week. Only do this if you want. You can use the following format if it's helpful.

    1. Try to write a record of at least one "good time" you had with your sibling.

    2. Also, write about at least two "hard times" you had.

In this diary, you can record what happened and your response to it. You can also write about possible actions you could take that might be more helpful the next time this happens.

1. A good time I had with my sibling this week was _____

_____

2. One hard time I had with my sibling this week was _____

_____

The way I responded was_____

_____

3. Another hard time I had with my sibling this week was _____

_____

The way I responded this time was _____

_____

Next time there is a hard time, I would like to respond by _____

PART THREE: **for kids
and parents**
stories about other families

activity 6
The Routines of Life

This book has stories about families where one of the children has ADHD. Some of the stories may sound like what happens in your family. However, people with ADHD have different personalities; as with all people, vast differences exist, and no one generalization defines an ADHD person. These differences in behavior result in both wonderful and difficult times between family members. As you read these stories, mark the parts that sound familiar to you.

Now read this story about Sarah and her family.

Sarah is eleven years old, and her brother, Johnny, is thirteen. In the morning, Sarah wakes up, gets dressed, comes downstairs for breakfast, and gets ready for school all by herself. She's ready to go when Dad is ready to drive them to school.

Johnny has more trouble. Johnny seems to slow down the whole family in the morning, and sometimes there's a lot of yelling about getting to school. Johnny just wants to stay in bed! So Mom goes into his room four or five times just to tell him to get out of bed and into his clothes. Then, instead of coming downstairs for breakfast, Johnny gets involved with his toys or his electronic games, and he takes forever.

Sarah gets so frustrated when Johnny's not ready—especially since she is all set to go and has to get to school to talk to a teacher. This is when Mom sometimes starts yelling.

"Johnny, I've reminded you five times to get going. When are you going to get down here?"

Then Johnny yells back at Mom, "I'll be there in a minute! Why are you always bugging me?"

In this way the morning becomes chaotic, with lots of yelling and anger.

Then, when Johnny finally does come downstairs, half the time he doesn't know where his stuff is! He runs around looking for his homework, his book bag, and especially his shoes. Sometimes Sarah tries to help look for Johnny's shoes, just because she doesn't want to be late for school.

Events

In Sarah's family, the morning is the hardest time of day, because Johnny is distracted and there's a lot of yelling.

Now it is your turn to think about your family times.

Circle the activities that can be upsetting or difficult for any of the people in your house:

Eating dinner	Doing homework	Sharing TV or video games	Choosing family activities
Cleaning the bedroom	Walking the dog	Clearing the table	Doing the dishes
Picking up toys off the floor	Brushing teeth	Riding in the car	Getting ready for bed
Waking up in the morning	Getting to school on time	Playing games together	

Write or talk with your parent(s) about what makes those times hard for you or your family members.

_____

_____

_____

Feelings

After thinking about the hard times of the day in her family, Sarah said:

> "Things in my family aren't fair! I feel angry and sad when there's so much yelling. Sometimes I just try to help out more because there's less yelling if I just do it. Mom and Dad give Johnny so much attention just to get him to do simple things like waking up and getting dressed. And then they only have a small amount of time left for me! It's frustrating because it never seems to change."

Now it's your turn to think about how you feel when the hard times happen.

Circle some of the feelings you might notice during the hard times of the day:

Sad	Nervous	Bored	Relieved
Silly	Hurt	Tired	Annoyed
Relaxed	Happy	Confused	Frustrated
Jealous	Excited	Angry	

You may have more than one feeling about hard times of the day. Sarah felt angry and sad and frustrated.

Think of each feeling as a different part of you, so that each feeling has a place in your thinking. So, for Sarah, one part of her felt sad when people yelled so much and another part felt angry.

The same could be true for you.

Let's use the bubbles below to list the feelings you might have marked on the previous page. The first bubble is an example of how to do the exercise, if one of your marked feelings was angry.

A part of me feels <u>angry</u>.

Important note for parents:

Here's your opportunity to let your child know you really understand the feelings they are experiencing—and that it's okay to have these feelings.

Check inside yourself and see what you understand about what your child is saying about their feelings.

Then let them know what you understand. For instance, "I do understand that when people raise their voices and seem out of control, it can be scary."

This way, hopefully, your child will feel understood.

Encourage your child to notice the vulnerable feelings, such as fear or sadness, that might precede anger or frustration.

The angry part feels this way because my parents and sibling end up yelling and arguing, which first scares and upsets me, and then I feel angry at them.

Let your *angry* part know that it's okay to feel angry with your sibling and perhaps even with your parents. And let it know that you understand why it feels angry. For instance, let it know that no one likes to hear his or her loved ones yelling. It's uncomfortable, and it even might feel scary. It probably doesn't seem fair that they don't control themselves better.

It's easier to feel anger, but you might feel scared or uncomfortable underneath the anger.

Now, fill in the second bubble with another feeling you circled above.

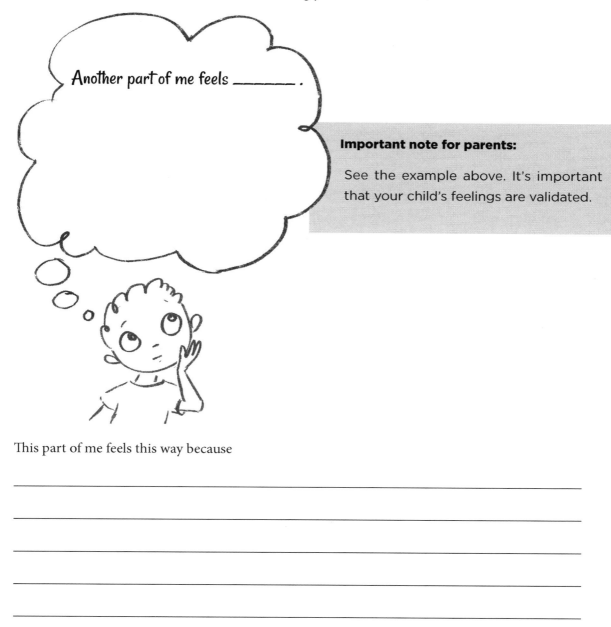

Another part of me feels _____ .

Important note for parents:

See the example above. It's important that your child's feelings are validated.

This part of me feels this way because

_____

_____

_____

_____

_____

Let your _____ part know that you understand why it feels this way.

If this part of you feels understood by your parent, and if it also feels understood and accepted by you, then it should feel good, and you should feel a sense of being understood and validated.

Did You Know...

ADHD has a lot to do with being able to control your own thoughts and actions.

Think about this: when you must stop watching TV and get ready for bed, you must do a lot of things!

- First you must stop watching TV—turn it off or walk away from it.

- Next you must leave the room, brush your teeth, go to your room, put on your pajamas, and get into bed.

- You'll have to stop doing something fun (watching TV) and start doing something more boring.

> Many kids with ADHD have trouble stopping fun things and starting boring things.

Kids with ADHD often get distracted. They might even start doing something else on their way to the bathroom. It's easy for them to get off track while they are trying to complete a task.

You might feel the person with ADHD just needs to try harder! But, strange as it sounds, your sibling is already trying hard to cooperate. Their brain just isn't making it easy. Your sibling's mind gets easily off track, so trying harder isn't always the solution. Sometimes kids have to learn to do things in different ways, but they need help to learn those ways.

What Can You Do?

Here are few ways you might help make those hard times easier:

- Offer to help your sibling when they're taking a long time to find things. Whether they say thanks or not, you may feel better being of help.

- Ask your mom or dad to teach your sibling to say "thanks" when you lend a hand.

- Don't give advice or tell your sibling what to do unless they welcome it. You're not the parent—and if you act like one, your sibling will probably either ignore you or resent you.

- If you feel like having a race, you can challenge your sibling to one—make it fun for them to get going. For instance, see who can get dressed faster in the morning. Many people with ADHD love competition and excitement; these can help their brains focus better and stay on task. It's not your job to speed your sibling up. It's your parents' challenge, so only have a race if you'll enjoy it, too.

- When you feel stressed, or when problems start to escalate, you can try removing yourself by walking away, Perhaps go to your room for a few minutes and distract yourself. You don't need to stand by and witness conflict if it doesn't involve you. If you can find a way to stay and be helpful to your sibling, that's fine, too.

- Let your mom or dad know when you're feeling frustrated, disappointed, or ignored. Letting people know how you feel prevents those feelings from building up inside you.

If you completed these pages on your own...

- Show your mom or dad the activities that you chose to do in this chapter.

- Talk about some of the difficult times when people do not follow the rules.

- Tell your parents what you are thinking and feeling when the rules are broken.

- Share some of the new facts you've learned about ADHD.

_____

_____

_____

activity 7
Respecting Rules

Now read this story about Emma and her family.

Emma's younger sister, Callie, gets away with a lot! Even if Emma tells Callie, "Don't go in my room," and even if their parents say the same thing, Callie still does it. Callie is just curious and almost doesn't seem to care if she gets in trouble. Callie may take Emma's clothes to "try them on" or to "borrow them." Callie sometimes "borrows" Emma's dolls and then leaves them everywhere around the house.

Emma feels that Callie is hardly ever punished. When Emma complains about how unfair things seem, her mom says, "Emma, I can't punish Callie for every little thing she does." But to Emma, these things don't seem little.

"My things get lost and sometimes ruined. They're important to me!" Emma cries to her mom. "And Callie always lies to you. She never admits that she takes my dolls. Plus, you never punish her for her lies and hardly ever punish her for taking my things!" Emma is sure that if she were caught lying, she'd get into big trouble with her mom.

Events

Check the boxes next to the rules that people often don't follow in your household:

☐ Turning off the TV or video games when asked.

☐ Not hitting.

☐ Telling the truth.

☐ Not taking things that belong to others.

☐ Not calling people names.

☐ Sharing generously with others.

Write about or talk with your parent about some other kinds of rules that are not followed in your household.

_____

_____

_____

What are the consequences if someone breaks the rules? (Some examples of consequences are losing TV time, going to bed early, having a time-out, not having playdates, or not getting dessert.)

_____

_____

_____

Do people get different consequences or punishments for breaking the same rules?

_____

_____

_____

_____

Are your consequences sometimes more serious than your sibling's?

_____

_____

_____

_____

Let's see how Emma feels about her situation:

> Emma is confused. Part of her wants to tell Mom every time Callie does something wrong, but another part of her doesn't want to be a tattletale. She just doesn't know the right thing to do. Emma feels angry that there are different rules and consequences for different kids. It just doesn't seem fair to her. She's mad at her mom but also feels bad that her mom has her hands full with Callie.

> Plus, Emma is afraid to have friends come over to play. She feels embarrassed by Callie's silly behaviors, and she knows that Callie won't be able to leave her alone to play with her friends. Emma is really frustrated, but she doesn't talk to her mom about it. She worries that if she tells her mom, then her mom will just have another problem to deal with—and might be more stressed.

> She wants her family to be less upset and less stressed. So one of her ways to try to make things easier for the family is to just be quiet about her feelings. Even if being quiet seems to be the best way, though, it still just doesn't seem fair.

Feelings

Put a check next to the confusing situations below that come up for you.

☐ I sometimes don't know when to tell my parents that my sibling is doing something wrong.

☐ When my sibling does something wrong, I worry what the consequences will be. I especially worry about how my parents will treat him or her.

☐ I sometimes feel I shouldn't bother my parents by telling them how I feel, especially if I'm sad, frustrated, or angry at my sibling.

☐ I don't think I should tell my parents that I'm angry at them.

☐ I don't know what to say to other kids about my brother or sister who has ADHD.

Try to discuss these and other confusing choices or situations with your parent. They may be helpful to you in sorting out your feelings and options.

Feelings You Notice When Your Sibling Has Trouble Respecting Rules

Circle the feelings you may have about your sibling and their actions when your sibling does not follow rules.

Frustration	Worry	Annoyance	Jealousy
Anger	Confusion	Lack of Concern	Sadness

What other feelings do you notice in yourself when your sibling does not follow rules?

_____

_____

_____

Write down or discuss with your parent the specific times you feel these emotions and what situations might cause them.

_____

_____

_____

_____

Fill in the bubble with one feeling you notice when your sibling has trouble following rules.

A part of me feels

_____ .

The events that lead to my feeling this way are

_____

_____

_____

_____

Let your _____ part know that you understand why it feels this way.

As an example, perhaps you noticed a part that feels jealous when your sibling breaks rules and seems to get away with it.

If your jealous part doesn't feel accepted and understood by you, then think about why not. Are there other parts of you that don't like the jealous part?

Maybe you're judging yourself and telling yourself that it's not right to feel jealous.

If so, ask that judging part whether it can relax. Let it know that jealousy is just a feeling— that everyone gets jealous and it's not bad.

Go back to the previous page. Fill in other thought bubbles with other feelings you circled, if you'd like. This may help you to really acknowledge those feelings.

Important note for parents:

Check your own reactions and see what you understand about what your child is saying. And then let your child know exactly what you understand.

Did You Know...

For you, following rules may come easily. That's why you may feel very angry when your sibling with ADHD doesn't follow rules well.

> Following rules means you often must stop yourself from doing things you want to do.

Kids like you are often angry that their parents are not punishing the child with ADHD more harshly. In fact, many kids are even angry because their parents just can't make the sibling with ADHD behave, period. But it's not just anger—many kids feel very sad at times. They feel sad when dinners or vacations get ruined or when people argue a lot.

> Since many ADHD kids have trouble stopping themselves, they may have a hard time following rules.

What Can You Do?

What can you do when your sibling is not following rules?

- You can tell your sibling exactly how you feel and why you feel that way.

  For instance, Emma could say:

  "Callie, when you take my dolls without asking me, my feelings get hurt. I feel like you don't care about me. If my things get broken, I feel sad. So please try to take better care of them."

- You can tell your parents exactly how you feel and why you feel that way.

  To her parents, Emma could say:

  "I feel like I don't have any private space, and I don't feel respected in this house, especially if you don't give Callie a consequence or make it up to me when my things are broken. I know it's difficult to control her, but at least either she or you should do something to make it up to me."

- You can ask for a family meeting so that rules can be made clearer.

- You can let your parents know that things seem unfair. Of course, life is not fair, but parents can try to make things as fair as possible in a family.

- You can also ask your parents to meet with a family counselor, a professional who helps families dealing with challenging situations.

If you completed these pages on your own...

- Show your mom or dad the activities that you chose to do in this chapter.

- Talk about some of the difficult times when people do not follow the rules.

- Tell your parents what you are thinking and feeling when the rules are broken.

- Share some of the new facts you've learned about ADHD.

_____

_____

_____

activity 8
Things Don't Seem Fair

Now read more about Emma and her family.

Emma has started to think that maybe she's just not that important. Her parents are always giving Callie a break. They hardly ever punish her, and they're always talking about Callie and her problems. Emma has begun to feel as if she has to be almost perfect, because she doesn't want to cause any more problems for her parents. She sees how stressed they are already.

She feels guilty if she asks for any of her mom's attention, because Mom seems so tired and Callie needs so much help. After all, Callie is having trouble at school, she doesn't have that many friends, and she isn't very nice to their parents.

A part of Emma is starting to tell her that she doesn't have a right to have any problems. Sometimes she feels sad about this, especially when she thinks that things will never change in her house. Emma sometimes wishes that Callie could go live somewhere else or go to a boarding school. Then, in the next moment, she feels bad for having those thoughts.

Events

The next activities will help you think about times of the day or situations that seem to be unfair.

Use the next exercises to identify your inner feelings. You can either write these things down or discuss them with your parent. Basically, you're trying to figure out what feelings you notice about your family, about your sibling, and about yourself.

The situation with my sibling that seems the most **unfair** is…

_____

_____

_____

_____

The times **I really need attention** but don't ask for it are (Examples might be when doing homework, when you have a problem with a friend, when you have some worries, or when you really want some special time with a parent):

_____

_____

_____

_____

Are there ways you try to be **extra-good** to make up for the issues your ADHD sibling has? (For example, by being a good student, by being well-behaved, or being extra helpful around the house.)

_____

_____

_____

_____

Circle the feelings you have about your family or sibling when things seem unfair in the household:

Guilt	Shame	Sadness	Protectiveness	Frustration
Anger	Worry	Disgust	Confusion	Disinterested

Are there *other* feelings you experience when things seem unfair?

_____

_____

_____

Do you sometimes feel it's difficult to tell your parents about how you feel when things seem unfair? If so, why?

_____

_____

_____

Did You Know...

People start to believe things about themselves or the world when they go through hard situations. Although these ideas seem right, they may not be true. You may get ideas like "I don't really deserve much attention" or "My feelings shouldn't matter" or "I have to be perfect so my family can be more normal." These things are not true, of course—but parts of you can start thinking things like this because you're going through such a hard time.

Think of it this way: If your sibling didn't have ADHD, and didn't have behavior problems, then wouldn't your parents probably have more attention to give to you? So it's not you. It's the situation —a challenging one for everyone. You still deserve the attention.

It's just a hard situation. There isn't as much attention available because one person happens to need more than usual. You still deserve the attention, and it's okay to wish for it. This is why kids and parents can be sad or hurt—because they know that people aren't always getting what they deserve and wish for.

Sometimes people feel as if two parts of themselves are pulling in opposite directions. It can make them tense or unhappy.

> Try to notice whether you have ideas or feelings about your family situation that are pulling you in opposite directions.

For instance, in this chapter, Emma has one part of her that's telling her she shouldn't have any problems. This part of her doesn't want to cause her parents any more stress. It thinks Emma should keep her frustrations to herself.

But another part of her feels things are not fair in her house, and this part would like her to speak out loudly about being sad and angry.

Emma feels the tension. At any one time, one feeling is usually stronger, and it takes over.

For instance, Emma might act as if everything is fine most of the time. However, if she gets very frustrated, then the angry part may take over. Usually if a part has been pushed down for a long time, when it does take over, it's loud or intense.

Try to notice whether you have ideas or feelings about your family situation that are pulling you in opposite directions.

This is common, because the situations in families where one person is struggling can become complicated.

Look at the feelings you circled earlier in this section. One part of you might be feeling protective of your sibling while another part might be feeling frustrated. These two feelings may pull you in opposite directions.

Make room for all the feelings you notice. They're all important. Also, notice what beliefs or ideas you may have about yourself, such as "I shouldn't burden my parents with my needs," "I don't need much attention; I'm fine," or "I'm mean because I often don't like my brother or sister." These kinds of thoughts or beliefs about yourself are important, too, even if they may not be correct or accurate.

What Can You Do?

Here are some ways to make things fairer for you:

- Tell yourself that you do deserve attention, even if your parent has to spend a lot of time focusing on your sibling with ADHD.

- Tell this to yourself over and over (or write it down and read it over and over).

- Tell yourself, "I am important. It's just that my brother or sister is having a lot of problems."

- Again, tell this to yourself often (write it down and read it over and over).

- Ask for support and attention from other adults, such as teachers, babysitters, uncles, aunts, cousins, and grandparents. Many kids get a lot of needs met by other adults who may have more energy and time than their parents.

- Tell yourself, "I have a right to ask for what I want."

- Be sure to ask for special time with your parents, when it's just you alone. Even small amounts of alone time with a parent can really help.

If you completed these pages on your own...

- Show your mom or dad the activities that you chose to do in this chapter.

- Talk about some of the difficult times when things don't seem fair in the family.

- Say what you are thinking and feeling when things are not fair for you.

- Share some interesting facts about ADHD you have learned from this chapter.

_____

_____

_____

activity 9
Getting Along with Others

Now read this story about Billy and his family.

Billy's older brother, Fred, can be a lot of fun, but he can be hard to get along with. Fred plays ball with Billy, which Billy really likes—until Fred starts to tease or goof around too much.

"Hey, Fred, don't throw the ball so far! It might go over the fence," yells Billy.

Then, just to tease him, Fred throws the ball really high—almost over the fence! Billy is frustrated and nearly bangs into the fence just to catch it.

Fred doesn't do anything for very long before he either wants to do some-thing different or else gets a little mean. He can't just play and enjoy it.

Fred is also sometimes in a bad mood, so Billy feels he has to watch out.

"I wonder if he'll put me in a headlock today," Billy thinks almost every day. Even though Fred isn't that much bigger, when he's mad, he can hit, push, or just torment Billy. Billy feels as if his parents really don't do anything to stop it.

Basically things pretty much have to be Fred's way, or else Fred gets mean. He'll yell, threaten, or hit. Billy usually just takes it or goes to his room, because there is no point fighting with Fred.

"If I fight with Fred," thinks Billy, "he just gets really mad and has to show he's the boss. That's when I might get hurt, or we will both get into trouble."

Events

In Billy's family, Fred's bad moods and bossiness often make playing together difficult. Fred will tease Billy or will need to change activities frequently.

Now it is your turn to think about how people get along in your own family. Check off some annoying behaviors that occur in your family:

☐ Interrupting   ☐ Talking too much

☐ Crying   ☐ Yelling

☐ Mimicking   ☐ Hitting

☐ Kicking   ☐ Criticizing

☐ Breaking things   ☐ Teasing

☐ Badgering (repeatedly asking for something, hoping the other person will just give in)

Who does these the most? You can write people's names next to the behaviors and give short examples, or write about what happens here:

_____

_____

_____

_____

Are there times when people get forceful or mean or must have their own way? If so, when does this happen, and who are the people involved?

_____

_____

_____

_____

How do you react when someone is very forceful or intense?

_____

_____

_____

_____

If you can't remember, check any of the boxes below that describe ways you choose to react. These are common ways that people react to pushiness.

☐   Submit or just go along

☐   Fight back

☐   Yell, cry, or make a fuss

☐   Make threats back at your sibling

☐   Call your sibling names

☐   Go along at first and then tell a parent

Are there other actions or behaviors that are annoying or worrisome in your family?

_____

_____

_____

_____

Feelings

How do you feel when someone acts very controlling, bossy, or intense?

An example might be when someone won't stop doing something to you or saying something to you that you don't like.

Check any of the boxes that apply to how you feel when someone acts this way:

☐	Scared	☐	Angry	☐	Amused
☐	Ashamed	☐	Resentful	☐	Uninterested
☐	Confused	☐	Sad	☐	impressed
☐	Trapped	☐	Disgusted	☐	Jealous

OR

Write about your feelings here:

_____

_____

_____

_____

_____

Did You Know...

Needing to change activities after only a short time can be frustrating to siblings, who may want to keep playing a game longer. Also, instead of changing to a new game, many kids who get bored will start to joke around, get silly, or maybe provoke their playmates in some way (such as making fun or teasing). This seems exciting to the person who is bored, but it is often frustrating to the person who is being teased or provoked.

> Many kids with ADHD get bored easily, so they may want to change activities often.

Some kids who have ADHD are also moody; their moods can often change quickly and for almost no reason.

It's hard for these kids and their siblings—because no one knows when someone's mood will change.

What Can You Do?

Here are some things to try when your sibling is hard to get along with:

- Speak up about what you don't like. Make it specific. Here are some examples:
  - "I don't like it when you start to goof around in the middle of a game. Can you just play with me for five more minutes? Then we can switch to something else."
  - "Maybe it's funny for you when you tease me, but it's not fun for me. It makes me really angry at you, so that I don't want to be around you."
  - "Mimicking me may feel good to you, but it's not fun for me. It makes me feel sad and annoyed at you."
- Take yourself to another room. Find another activity to do that doesn't involve your sibling. If you separate yourself, your sibling may get the message that you don't want to play unless he or she is nice.
- Discuss the situation with your parents. Let them know that you need some help trying to figure out how to get along with your sibling.
- Suggest games or activities to play with your sibling that may keep his or her interest longer.
- Arrange playdates or activities with your friends so that you can have time away from your sibling. This gives everyone a needed break.
- Ask your mom or dad to arrange for family therapy with a counselor who can help with these problems.

If you completed these pages on your own...

• Show your mom or dad the activities that you chose to do in this chapter.

• Talk about some of the difficult times when people aren't getting along.

• Tell your parents what you're thinking and feeling when people aren't getting along.

• Share some interesting facts about ADHD you have learned from this chapter.

_____

_____

_____

activity 10
It's Hard to Have a Conversation

Now read some more about Billy and his family.

At dinner, Fred always has to talk and be the center of attention. Mom and Dad ask him to be quieter and to let others talk, but it's really hard for Fred. He just says whatever is on his mind. For instance, Fred interrupts Billy almost every time Billy tries to talk about his day. Sometimes it's really funny, but a lot of times, it's just annoying.

Billy is used to the way Fred is, but it makes him sad. It's almost as if Fred is the only important one, and Billy wonders if maybe he's not that important.

Conversations—What Happens?

Are there times when your sibling interrupts a lot?

☐ **YES**　　　☐ **NO**

If you checked yes, write down what you do when you are interrupted:

_____

_____

If a parent is there when you are interrupted, what does your parent do?

_____

_____

_____

How do you feel about what your parent does? Is it fair?

_____

_____

_____

Does it seem as though your sibling has trouble sharing the spotlight?

☐ **YES**　　　☐ **NO**

Conversations—Feelings

What about your feelings when you're interrupted or can't get any attention?

Check the feelings that you notice when you're interrupted or when someone else just takes over the spotlight.

☐ Disrespected   ☐ Frustrated

☐ Annoyed   ☐ Angry

☐ Hurt   ☐ Intimidated

☐ Sad   ☐ Relieved

☐ Jealous   ☐ Hopeless

☐ Unimportant   ☐ Detached

Write down any other feelings you notice when you're interrupted or when someone else grabs the spotlight.

_____

_____

_____

A part of me feels _____.

Fill out the next two bubbles with the two strongest feelings you checked on the list above.

A. This part of me feels this way because _____.

Let your _____ part know that you understand why it feels this way.

> Another part of me feels _____ .

Important note for parents:

Here's another opportunity to validate your child's feelings. Try to understand what their position is and let them know you understand.

B. This part of me feels this way because _____.

Let your _____ part know that you understand why it feels this way.

See if your _____ part feels accepted by you or cared about by you.
Check inside yourself to see.

Did You Know...

One kind of action might be playing ball, even in the house; another might be playing video games. Another might be the need to keep suggesting new things to do or to joke or tease.

> Many kids with ADHD feel bored a lot and need almost constant action.

What about Interrupting or Talking a Lot?

Another kind of action is talking. Many kids with ADHD will tend to just say whatever comes to mind, even if they are interrupting others.

When kids don't share well or wait their turn, they aren't thinking through how it will make others feel. These kinds of actions are called "impulsive." Someone has a thought, and they just act on it without really thinking through whether it's a good idea or not. So controlling one's actions and regulating one's behavior can be hard for many ADHD kids.

For other ADHD kids, it's hard to get into action of any kind. They may seem lazy or unmotivated. They also may get distracted by their own thoughts, so that they can seem "spacey," as if they are in their own world a lot.

What Can You Do?

What can you do when you are interrupted or when someone else needs to grab the spotlight?

- You can say, "Excuse me; I was still talking. Please wait for me to finish!"

- You can say, "That's the third time you interrupted me at dinner. Please just let me say something. I'm important too."

- You can appeal to your parents. "Mom, I would like to have a chance to talk about my day. A lot happened, and so far we've only been hearing about my sibling's day. Doesn't everyone get a chance in this family?"

- You can ask to talk to a parent separately so that you won't be interrupted by your sibling. You can explain to your parent that this is important to you.

- At a family meeting, you can suggest that each person have five minutes at dinner to tell about his or her day.

- Again, you can ask your parents to see a family counselor who can meet with the whole family—or perhaps just with the siblings—to help you work out better ways to get along.

If you completed these pages on your own...

- Show your mom or dad the activities that you chose to do in this chapter.

- Talk about the difficult times when people are interrupting or talking too much.

- Tell your parent what you're thinking and feeling when a conversation is not going well.

- Share some of the facts you have learned about ADHD in this chapter.

_____

_____

activity 11
Struggling with Self-Control

Now read this story about Sandy and her family.

Sandy's younger brother, Ricardo, is so loud she can hardly stand it. When Mom is on the phone, it always seems as though Ricardo needs something —and he needs it right then. He can never wait, so he keeps interrupting Mom louder and louder until she has to pay attention. If Mom answers him, he's quiet for a little while. If Mom says that he has to wait, he just has a big tantrum, so it's not even worth it to Mom.

When Sandy and Ricardo watch TV, Ricardo is always getting silly and excited. That would be okay, except he starts jumping on the couch that they are both sitting on.

Basically, Ricardo constantly gets carried away. He's either excited or mad or just demanding until he gets what he wants.

The other side of Ricardo is that when he's happy, he can help everyone be in a good mood. He can be so happy or so funny—like when he's imitating a teacher—that the whole family laughs so hard that they can't stop.

Sandy is sometimes annoyed, sometimes amused, and often just doesn't know what to do. Sometimes she corrects Ricardo, sounding like a parent when she tells him how to behave or to stop doing what he's doing. Ricardo doesn't usually listen to Sandy then, and he's often annoyed at her for correcting him.

Self-Control—What Happens?

Check the boxes next to the behaviors listed below that happen in your family, and answer the other questions about those behaviors.

Controlling one's body:

☐   Jumping when others are still

☐   Running around more than others

☐   Tapping or making other noises

Who does these things? Where? When?

_____

_____

_____

Needing attention right away:

☐   Having to go first and not taking turns very well

☐   Interrupting when others are talking or on the phone

☐   Being very loud so others will listen

☐   Needing to get one's own way, even if it means being very demanding

☐   Having trouble compromising

☐   Needing to know everything about everyone else's business and insisting on being told, even if it's not his or her business

Who has these traits?

_____

_____

_____

Trouble respecting personal space and other people's feelings:

☐   Poking others when they want to be left alone

☐   Grabbing things that others have or will want soon, like a TV remote or video-
game controller

☐   Going into another person's room without permission

☐   Teasing or provoking

☐   Getting carried away

☐   Getting very silly

Who does these things in your family?

_____

_____

_____

How do you react when these things happen?

_____

_____

_____

Self-Control—Feelings

Circle the different feelings you notice in yourself when your sibling has trouble with self-control:

Excited	Annoyed	Jealous	Confused
Frustrated	Playful	Angry	Critical
Sad	Unconcerned	Worried	Disgusted

OR

Write about how you feel when your sibling has trouble with self-control:

_____

_____

Again, notice that you may have more than one feeling when someone has trouble with self-control.

A part of me feels _____ .

Another part of me feels _____ .

We can call each feeling a different part of you, so that each feeling has a place in your thinking.

In the two bubbles to the left, write down two of the feelings that you circled above.

Important note for parents:

Here's another chance for your child to feel really understood by you. Don't hesitate to ask questions about how and what your child feels or experiences.

In the top bubble, this _____ part feels this way because (give examples of what happens to provoke your feelings) _____.

Let your _____ part know that you understand why it feels what it feels.

In the bottom bubble, this _____ part feels this way because (give examples of what happens to provoke your feelings) _____.

Let your _____ part know that you understand why it feels what it feels.

As an example, perhaps you noticed a part that gets angry when people don't show good self-control.

If it doesn't feel okay to you to feel angry, then you're not feeling accepting of your angry part. Try to sense why not. Are there parts of you that think it's not okay to feel angry or to have a part of you that feels angry?

Maybe you're judging yourself and telling yourself that you shouldn't feel angry.

If so, ask that judging part whether it can relax. Let it know that anger is just a feeling that everyone gets—and that it's not bad.

> **Important note for parents:**
>
> Help your child with this exercise so that both you and your child can really be sure that all of these parts [feelings] are welcome and are accepted as a normal part of being alive.

Did You Know...

As we've discussed before, there are many ways kids with ADHD have trouble with self-control.

Many kids with ADHD have trouble controlling their feelings. Their feelings are often intense and very strong. And the feelings often occur quickly, taking the children by surprise. It's not only that the feelings are strong; many kids with ADHD are also impulsive or act without having the time to think. Many kids with ADHD tend to be loud, get easily frustrated, and then get pushy because they want their way so badly.

Many kids know, and can even say later, that they're being unfair. But the biggest problem with ADHD is that kids *can't help doing the things they do.* This is really frustrating for them. Sometimes they can help it, and those are the times when their behavior is fine. But sometimes they can't help it. Your brother or sister may not apologize very well

> Underneath, kids who have trouble with their behavior often feel ashamed that it's so hard to them to act in a fair or caring way.

or may not want to admit that he or she was unfair, but almost all kids wish they could be thoughtful and caring. The frustration of having ADHD is that one can't always act that way. And don't be fooled—even a kid who seems happy with how they act isn't really as happy as they look.

Underneath, kids who have trouble with their behavior often feel ashamed that it's so hard for them to act in a fair or caring way.

As a brother or sister who sees their sibling having trouble with their behavior, you may feel very tempted to correct them or tell them to stop doing something or to start doing something they're supposed to do. Since this is a parent's job, your sibling probably won't listen to your suggestion. They also may be quite annoyed that you're stepping in and sounding like a parent, when really you are just another kid.

What Can You Do?

- Have a sense of humor. Laughing, even about upsetting things, can help your family.

- Being silly when you're mad often can help you as well as your sibling. Since ADHD kids do so many things "wrong," they're often defensive. They often don't admit to problems or mistakes.

- Your job isn't to pretend that there aren't problems—but the more you can be relaxed about them, the easier it will be.

- Talk to your parents about ways of getting space, if that is what you need. Go to a friend's house to get a break.

- If your sibling is invading your personal space, move to another chair.

- Again, ask for a family meeting to raise an issue. For example, if your sibling has taken any of your belongings, you can ask to have them returned to you. When things feel unfair, you could ask for some special time with a parent or a special privilege that would make things feel better.

If you completed these pages on your own...

- Show your mom or dad the activities that you chose to do in this chapter.

- Talk about some of the difficult times when people aren't controlling themselves.

- Tell your parent what you are thinking and feeling when this happens.

- Share some ideas you have about how much your sibling can or can't control their actions.

_____

_____

_____

activity 12
Feelings, Actions, and Reactions

Now read more about Sarah and her family.

Remember Sarah's brother, Johnny? In their family, when Mom gets really frustrated at Johnny, she first starts nagging him.

"Johnny, I've asked you to get dressed four times already. You've got to get moving."

Then Mom's tone gets more frustrated and harsh.

"Johnny, what am I going to have to do to get you down here? I've really had it. You might miss the bus, and I don't have time to drive you to school today."

Finally, Mom just yells at Johnny.

"Johnny, I've really had it. You're going to lose TV for a week. You're just not cooperating, and I'm sick of it!"

Then Johnny often yells back. "Why is everyone always picking on me? I just couldn't find my shoes. I said I'd be right down. No one cares about me in this house."

Sometimes Sarah starts yelling at Johnny, too. "Johnny, hurry up! Why can't you listen?"

Or if she gets really mad, she might say something mean, like "Why are you so stupid?" or "You're such a pain!"

Once one person is having trouble being in control, then others start to nag, yell, hit, or threaten in order to get the kid with ADHD to behave well. Pretty soon everyone in the family is yelling, shutting themselves in their rooms, or getting upset.

Sarah hates to hear her mom start to get irritated with Johnny. She never knows when Johnny might just blow up or whether Mom will blow up first. Then she has to worry if they'll be late for school. And she doesn't feel good after she calls Johnny a name, either.

Many times it's the way everyone gets so upset that leads to difficult feelings—like anger, jealousy, sadness, hopelessness, worry, or a desire to run away.

Another common feeling you may experience is the sense that your ADHD sibling gets all the attention. You might feel things like:

"I'm hurt because I'm being ignored."

"I'm jealous of all the attention my sibling gets. Even though my mom is yelling at my brother, I feel as if she doesn't even notice me."

"I'm angry at my sibling—and at my parents! Can't they find a way to get along better?"

"I'm sad at this whole unhappy situation!"

All these feelings or parts of you can be happening at nearly the same time. So take a couple of deep breaths, let yourself just focus for a few moments, and notice which of these feelings happen for you. Take a moment to really acknowledge each one. Let each part of you know you see it and can make room for it.

You may also feel that you have to help your parents by taking care of yourself and not burdening them with any needs—including not telling them about your feelings. However, it's important to try to let them know how you feel. Although this can be a challenge, everyone will feel closer.

Expressing Emotions—How People Act

Actions are things people do, such as helping, interrupting, yelling, and teasing. They include things people say as well as things they do with their hands and feet.

Think about the answers to these questions. Then write about it or talk to your parents about it. When my sibling upsets me, I usually...

_____

_____

_____

_____

If my sibling hits me, I...

_____

_____

_____

_____

If I want to get my sibling into trouble, I…

_____

_____

_____

_____

If my sibling comes into my room without permission, I…

_____

_____

_____

_____

The ways I act toward my sibling that are upsetting or disappointing to me are…

_____

_____

_____

_____

Are there people in your family who have trouble with self-control? Below are some statements for you to think about.

People who act very angry in my family include:

_____

_____

_____

People who act very impatient in my family include:

_____

_____

_____

People who become overly excited in my family include:

_____

_____

_____

Are there people in your family who act pushy or demanding to get their own way? If so, who are they, and how do they act in a demanding way?

_____

_____

_____

What other kinds of feelings get expressed very strongly in your house?

By your sibling?

_____

_____

By other people?

_____

_____

Expressing Emotions—Feelings

How does it feel when people express themselves in a way that seems too strong to you?

Circle the feelings you notice in yourself when people express themselves in a way that seems too strong—that is, too intense or too "in your face."

Scared	Annoyed	Worried
Confused	Not bothered	Concerned
Amused	Sad	Frustrated
Angry	Want to get away	Want to argue

OR

Write how you feel when this happens:

_____

_____

_____

_____

_____

_____

_____

Pick one feeling you circled on the chart on the previoius page and fill in the bubble below.

When people in my family express feelings that are too strong for me,

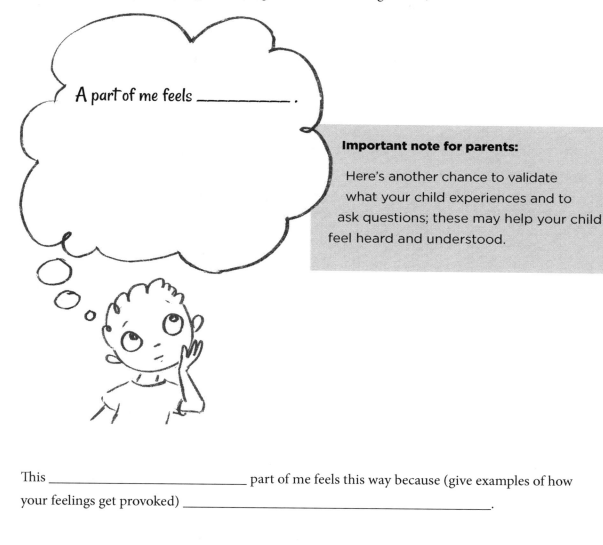

A part of me feels _____ .

Important note for parents:

Here's another chance to validate what your child experiences and to ask questions; these may help your child feel heard and understood.

This _____ part of me feels this way because (give examples of how your feelings get provoked) _____ .

Let your _____ part know that you understand why it feels the way it feels.

Did You Know...

Many kids with ADHD get very angry when they're frustrated.

What about your own feelings? What if you had trouble controlling your feelings? How might you act if your feelings were very strong and took over? Would you yell, grab, or hit?

Many kids with ADHD get overwhelmed when they're frustrated. They might act angry or pushy. Often they feel as if they need to get their way right away. They can't wait. Sometimes they get sad, seemingly over ordinary things, or they get excited and act a little out of control. Many ADHD kids sometimes frighten, hit, or hurt their siblings .

> Many kids with ADHD get very angry when they're frustrated.

When people get upset and have very strong feelings in your family, do other people sometimes get hurt?

Think of a time when you were hurt by your sibling.

_____

_____

_____

Did you tell a parent? If so, how did your parent react?

_____

_____

_____

And this is very important: do your parents believe you or take you seriously about how much you may get hurt by your sibling?

_____

_____

_____

What Can You Do?

- Ask your parent or sibling to speak in a calmer voice. You could say the following:

  - "I can't think straight when you yell."

  - "Mom, I wish you wouldn't yell. I don't think it's making my sibling go any faster anyway."

  - "I feel upset when you yell. Can you please try not to yell?"

- You can walk away or go to your room if people are making threats or talking loudly. And you're less likely to start yelling yourself. (It is not your job to fix things in your family. Also, when people are upset, they don't listen very well.)

- After an incident is over, when people are calmer, you can ask your sibling or your parent if there is something you can do to help. (Again, it's not your job to fix things, but you might feel like doing something easy that might help.)

- Again, try not to correct or reprimand your sibling when they're not acting correctly. Since you're not the parent, your sibling probably won't follow your orders—and will likely resent you for stepping in and sounding like a parent. Instead, express your wish. You could say, "I have a hard time thinking when you're so loud. Can you please be quieter?" Or "I hope you'll be ready soon. I really don't want to be late for school because I have a test."

- Ask your parents to call a family meeting. People could try to calmly discuss how to get along better. In the meeting, you can let everyone know how much the yelling upsets you.

- If family meetings don't help or your parents don't organize one, you could ask your parents if the family can go to a family counselor. A family counselor can help everyone communicate more kindly and calmly.

If you completed these pages on your own...

- Show your mom or dad the activities that you chose to do in this chapter.

- Talk about some of the difficult times when people aren't controlling their feelings and their actions.

- Say what you think and feel when this happens.

- Again, remember: it's your parents' job to make the family feel safe and comfortable.

- Share some new facts you may have learned about ADHD.

_____

_____

_____

PART FOUR: **for kids and parents**

moving forward

We've been talking about ways in which the brains of children with ADHD can make it hard to do what teachers, parents, or coaches expect of them. Though their actions may make it seem otherwise, the truth is that your sibling wants to fit in and to do the "right thing" most of the time. Remember that most ADHD kids develop much better self-control as they grow up. There are probably times when you have fun with your sibling, and you'll probably enjoy them more as you both get older.

It's normal to feel angry about your situation and to think that it's unfair to have sibling with ADHD. So you'll need some support. You can ask your parents for alone time, just one-on-one with them. If your parent is sometimes too stressed to be able to comfort you, try a grandparent, an aunt or uncle, a coach, a teacher, or any older person who can listen and comfort you. Sometimes, you can even go to a friend's house, where it might be calmer. You may find that you're not the only one with a challenging sibling!

Do you ever feel like you need to take care of your parent? If they are upset or crying, it's okay to give them a hug. But taking care of your parent is not your job. If they are upset, or argue often, you might ask if the whole family can go to a counselor together. It's healthy to get help when faced with difficult challenges.

Sometimes kids in your situation can be hard on themselves. You may even try to be extra cooperative to relieve stress in the family. If you try really hard to be different from your sibling, you might even feel a need to be perfect. Perhaps you want your parents to be really proud of you—or may just want things to go smoothly, for a change. Just remember that it's okay for you to have needs and occasional meltdowns, too.

If you feel embarrassed about your sibling when you're around other kids, just tell them that your sibling has challenges, and is working on them. When your sibling is doing something annoying, it's hard to stay calm. You know that telling them to stop probably won't help, so occasionally you'll lose your temper. This is human nature. Just see if you can use some of the strategies we talked about in the earlier activities in this book, under the "What Can You Do" sections.

You might ask your parents to agree on one or two rules to enforce. For example, you could request that your sibling not enter your room without permission. As a family, you can agree on a clear consequence. Too many rules can be overwhelming to everyone, so think about one or two that will make a difference to you. You'll develop many strengths from having a challenging sibling, including patience and understanding. Most importantly, you'll learn how to appreciate everyone's differences.

In my many years of working with families I've come to understand that compassion, acceptance, and humor go a long way to soothing the wounds of frustration and hurt. I'm hopeful that this book can serve as a resource that will help reduce shame and tension in your family. And remember to have fun creating strategies that work for you.

PART FIVE: appendices

Appendix I: For Kids and Parents
If Your Brother or Sister Takes Medication for ADHD

Appendix II: For Kids and Parents
Summary and Review Sheets from
Our Stories about Other Families

Appendix III
Resources for Parents about ADHD

appendix 1
Medication

If your brother or sister takes medication for ADHD:

Parents try many ways to help children with ADHD behave more cooperatively and effectively, both at home and at school. They may use point systems, prizes, sticker charts, time outs and other tools to help encourage effectiveness at getting things done and getting along with others.

Remember, we all count on our brains to help us concentrate on tasks, ignore distractions, keep our emotions in check and follow through to get things done.

Also, recall that the brains of children with ADHD have some very positive qualities. Their brains often help them be more curious, creative, funny, or full of energy than many other kids.

However, the parts of their brains that help them focus, stay calm, and think before acting may be a little quieter, not as energized to keep them focused and stay in control.

This is where medication can sometimes help. Some young people with ADHD may take medication to energize these parts of their brains.

Then, with the help of medication they often have more capacity to behave cooperatively or be more successful at school.

Remember the children we got to know earlier in the book? One had trouble concentrating on and finishing his homework.

Fred had trouble listening at dinner. He couldn't wait quietly while others talked. He had to be the center of attention.

Ricardo was very restless and impulsive. He had trouble sitting still on the couch to watch TV, and he couldn't stop himself from interrupting his mom when she was on the phone.

Callie was so curious about her sister's toys, that she could not stop herself from going into Emma's room and taking apart her dollhouse.

So How Can Medication Help?

Medication can help the whole brain work more effectively.

Medicine, usually a pill or liquid, can actually help kids:

1. Concentrate longer on homework

2. Be more patient, while waiting their turn

3. Finish chores

4. Act calmer, less pushy or angry

5. Take more notice about what other people are feeling.

6. Be more thoughtful of other people

Medication can often help some children with ADHD behave in more considerate ways. They can more easily follow rules, respect other people's property, wait their turn, and feel calmer.

This is great for ADHD kids who are helped by medication, and it's great for their families. If your sibling does take medication, it probably is helping them with some of these problems.

But not all children with ADHD are helped by or use medication. One problem with some medications for ADHD is that they don't last all day. If a child takes medication in the morning, it might wear off by the afternoon or evening.

For Ricardo, pictured in Activity 11, his sister notices that he's calmer and pretty well behaved when he comes home from school. However, by about 5pm, Ricardo is louder and jumping around more. Once his medication wears off, self-control is more difficult for him.

Callie, Emma's little sister from Activity 7, only takes medication on school days. It helps Callie behave better at school, but Emma wishes that she could take medication on weekends, too. That's when she has to be with her sister the most.

Callie does not break the rules so much when she takes medication. It's just that Callie doesn't eat very well when she takes medication. It lowers her appetite. Callie was losing some weight, so she had to stop the medication on weekends.

This is frustrating for Emma, but there isn't much she can do, except try to use the strategies we listed at the end of Activity 7.

One Important Rule to Keep in Mind

If your sibling is acting up or upsetting you, do not say to them, "Did you take your medication today?"

It is a good question, and your parent would want to know the answer to it. But most kids feel annoyed and insulted if you ask them that. It probably sounds like you are accusing them of something, and kids just don't like it.

You could ask your parent if your sibling has taken their medication, if you are concerned or just want to know why they might be having a hard day. Just don't ask it in front of your brother or sister. They will feel criticized and singled out.

One Thing to Know About the Future:

Your sibling may not always take medication. Many kids outgrow aspects of their ADHD as they get older. Also, many kids just get better at learning how to manage and control their ADHD tendencies. Hopefully, your sibling is learning new strategies, just as you are trying to do by reading this book.

appendix 2
For Kids and Parents

Summary and Review Sheets From Our Stories About Other Families.

Each of the following summaries highlights the main points from the stories and exercises found in activities 6 through 12.

For your own use, you may photocopy or download and print these "Summary and Review Sheets" from the web at *www.ADHDSiblingChallenge.com/resources.* They may help remind you about what you've learned from this book. Try to refer to them when situations arise that seem frustrating or confusing.

Under "FEELINGS: How do you feel?", there are some examples of troubling or upsetting feelings you may have. However, you may also not feel especially bothered or upset by these events. At times you may have positive feelings, such as compassion or concern for your sibling as well as for other family members, even if they are having a hard time. At times some behaviors may just seem humorous or cute.

So, some events may be easy to ignore; others may create more discomfort for you.

The "WHAT CAN YOU DO" sections will remind you about helpful steps you can take to make things work better for you and for others and to enjoy your family more.

The Routines of Life: (see ACTIVITY 6, page 33)

Events: What are the signs that ADHD is interfering with following routines?

- Kids get distracted, taking longer to do things.

- People forget items they need, then take longer to find their things, such as shoes or homework.

- Kids get into arguments riding in the car. Kids with ADHD have a hard time with frustration.

Feelings: How do you feel?

- You may feel positive or neutral feelings, as mentioned on the preceding page.

- You may feel frustrated that things are unfair, and annoyed when your routine is disrupted.

Did You Know: How does ADHD make routines challenging for your sibling?

- Switching from one activity to another is often difficult, especially if they have to stop something that's fun and start something more boring.

- So, for instance, it can be hard to clean up after playing a game, or hard to turn off the TV and start doing homework.

- Kids with ADHD easily lose track and get distracted, when routines have several steps.

What Can You Do:

- Get some space when you feel stressed.

- Help your sibling out, but request that they say "Thank you."

- Only give advice if your sibling can accept it.

Respecting Rules: (see ACTIVITY 7, page 40)

Events: What are the signs that ADHD is interfering with respecting rules?

- Your sibling borrows your things without permission.

- Your sibling doesn't admit they have done something wrong.

- Your sibling doesn't follow other household rules.

Feelings: How do you feel?

- Again, you may feel neutral, understanding, or just not bothered when some rules are broken.

- You may feel frustrated or angry when your things get taken without permission.

- You sometimes feel that punishments aren't given out fairly, that your sibling "gets away with too much."

- You might feel confused about how much to complain to your parents.

Did You Know: ADHD makes respecting rules challenging for your sibling.

- ADHD makes it hard to stop yourself from doing something.

- ADHD kids can be impulsive. They seem to act without thinking.

- Once they have broken a rule, they might not admit it. Many kids with ADHD have trouble telling the truth about something they have done.

What Can You Do:

- Tell your sibling exactly how you feel when they don't respect your belongings or don't follow other rules.

- Tell your parents exactly how you feel and why you feel that way when your sibling doesn't follow rules.

- Ask for a family meeting so that rules can be made clearer.

- Let your parents know that things don't seem fair to you.

- Ask your parents if the family can meet with a family counselor to get more help with making things fairer

Things Don't Seem Fair: (see ACTIVITY 8, page 47)

Events: What are the signs that ADHD is interfering with things feeling fair?

- Your sibling is often the focus of your parents' attention.

- There are so many problems with your sibling that you think you shouldn't add any burdens to your parents.

- You think that your needs aren't very important.

- You keep many feelings to yourself.

Feelings: How do you feel?

- You may not feel concerned or bothered by these patterns.

- You may feel sad that your sibling gets so much attention and that your needs are being ignored.

- You could feel helpless.

- You might wish your sibling could live somewhere else.

- You may feel that you'd better be perfect, so you don't add to your parents' burdens.

Did You Know: ADHD makes it hard for your parents to keep things balanced and fair.

- Kids with ADHD have difficulty following rules and routines, and with self control.

- Parents have trouble helping kids with ADHD learn these skills.

- Until your sibling can learn these skills, things will not be balanced in your family. Your sibling will need extra care.

What Can You Do:

- Tell yourself:

  1. I deserve attention, even if my parent can't provide it immediately.

  2. I am important, but my sibling is having problems right now.

  3. I have a right to ask for what I want.

- Ask for:

  1. Support and attention from other adults, like teachers, uncles, aunts, family friends, babysitters, and grandparents.

  2. One-on-one time with your parents.

Getting Along With Others: (see ACTIVITY 9, pg 52)

Events: What are the signs that ADHD is interfering with getting along with others?

- Your sibling teases or goofs around, just when things are going well.

- Your sibling doesn't play things for very long before having to give up or make a change in the rules.

- Your sibling might be very moody.

- Your sibling has to have their own way.

Feelings: How do you feel?

- You may feel concern or compassion that your sibling is having a hard time.

- It's sometimes frustrating when someone just stops an activity suddenly or interrupts it by goofing around.

- You may feel scared and angry if your sibling becomes mean, disrupts your fun, or physically hurts you.

Did You Know: ADHD makes getting along difficult for your sibling.

- Becoming bored easily makes it hard to keep doing many activities, even ones that seem like they are fun to you.

- Some kids with ADHD have trouble controlling their aggression. They may think it's fun to hurt you or scare you.

- Some kids with ADHD are very moody. Their feelings and moods change quickly, making it hard for them to control themselves.

What Can You Do:

- Speak up about what you don't like. Be specific, such as "Mimicking may be fun for you, but it's not for me."

- Take yourself to another room and find another activity to do.

- Discuss the situation with your parents, so they can try to help you find solutions.

- Suggest games or activities that will keep your sibling's attention longer.

- Arrange play dates or visits with other kids, so you can have time away from your brother or sister.

It's Hard to Have a Conversation: (see ACTIVITY 10, page 58)

Events: What are the signs that ADHD is interfering with having a conversation?

- Your brother or sister almost always dominates the conversation.

- Your sibling interrupts you when you try to talk.

Feelings: How do you feel?

- You may not feel concerned, or might be understanding.

- You might feel cut off, disrespected, annoyed or helpless.

- You may think that there is no place for you or your ideas.

Did You Know: How ADHD can affect conversations?

- Many kids with ADHD need almost constant action, and talking is a kind of action.

- ADHD kids who are impulsive often act without thinking about how their actions might affect others.

- Your sibling might not realize that you feel so cut off or disrespected.

What Can You Do:

- You can say, "Excuse me! I was talking. Please wait for me to finish."

- You can say to your parent, "Mom, I would like to have a chance to talk about my day, too."

- You can ask a parent to talk with you separately, so that you can't be interrupted.

- At a family meeting, you can suggest that each person have five minutes at dinner to talk about their day.

Struggling with Self Control: (see ACTIVITY 11, page 64)

Events: What are the signs that ADHD is affecting your sibling's self-control?

- Your sibling needs what they want "right now." They can't wait.

- Your sibling gets very worked up with excitement, with anger, or with sadness. They express their feelings very intensely.

- Your sibling's feelings are so intense that they actually disrupt the family.

Feelings: How do you feel when your sibling gets carried away?

- Again, you may not feel bothered by these events or might also feel concern.

- You might feel annoyed at your sibling's loudness or insistence on getting what they want right away.

- It may often feel unfair to you, but you could also feel helpless to change things.

Did You Know: How does ADHD make it hard for your sibling to have self-control?

- Kids with ADHD often have feelings that are very strong and intense.

- Kids with ADHD have feelings that get strong very, very quickly, so they are hard to control.

- Kids with ADHD often feel that they need to get their way immediately. They have trouble waiting.

- However, kids with ADHD often feel ashamed that they have trouble controlling their feelings and actions. They wish they could act like other kids.

What Can You Do:

- Have a sense of humor.

- Try being silly, even when you are mad. Lightness and humor help everyone deal with upsetting times.

- Talk to your parents about ways of getting space. Maybe go to a friend's house to get a break.

Feelings, Actions, Reactions: (see ACTIVITY 12, page 71)

Events: When kids with ADHD delay or dawdle, families can have a lot of conflict.

- When kids with ADHD dawdle or procrastinate, parents often start to nag.

- After nagging a few times, parents often start to yell. Then kids with ADHD often yell back.

- Sometimes siblings join in to lecture or yell at their brother or sister who isn't doing something correctly.

Feelings: How do you feel?

- You may feel angry at your sibling with ADHD for not cooperating.

- You could feel angry and upset with your parent, if they are raising their voice and yelling at your sibling.

- You may feel very sad that your family has these struggles.

- You may worry about how people will recover from these arguments.

- You may not find these behaviors bothersome. They may be easy to ignore.

Did You Know:

- Many kids with ADHD get very overwhelmed when they are frustrated.

- They might act angrily or in a pushy way.

- Parents who don't feel listened to also tend to have trouble controlling their emotions. They often yell or make threats.

- People feel very stressed by arguing and tension in their home, including you.

What Can You Do:

- Tell your parent, "I feel upset when you yell. Can you please try not to yell?"

- Walk away or go to your room if people are raising their voices.

- Later, you can ask your sibling if there is anything you can do to help?

- It's not your job to fix things, but it can feel really good to offer to help.

- Try not to correct your sibling when they are not acting correctly. Perhaps say, "I hope you'll be ready soon for school. I have a test today and don't want to be late. Thanks."

appendix 3
Resources for Parents

CHADD.ORG

Children and Adults with Attention Deficit/Hyperactivity Disorder

CHADD is a non-profit organization that provides support and groups, community resource information, monthly meetings and more. Website has fact sheets, online communities, and many other resources.

ADDitude MAGAZINE

Additudemag.org

Magazine as well as online webinars, forums, blogs, and other resources.

UNDERSTOOD.ORG

Excellent resource for Learning Disabilities and ADHD. Founded by 15 non-profit organizations.

Attention Deficit Disorder Association (ADDA)

ADDA.org

Worldwide non-profit adult ADD organization.

Learning Disabilities Association

LDAamerica.org

LDA provides support to people with learning disabilities, their parents, teachers and other professionals.

National Resource Center on ADHD

Help4ADHD.org

National clearinghouse for science-based information about all aspects of Attention deficit/ hyperactivity disorder (ADHD)

Sibling Support Project

SiblingSupport.org

Sponsors "Sibshop" peer support groups nationwide as well as online.

An organization dedicated to helping siblings of children with special health, developmental, and mental health concerns.

Add Resources

AddResources.org

Find ADHD-related topics including assessment/testing, coping skills, relationships, diet and nutrition and more.

American Association of Child and Adolescent Psychiatry

AACAP.org

ADHD Resource Center

American Academy of Pediatricians

HealthyChildren.org

Understanding ADHD: Information for Parents

Child Mind Institute

ChildMind.org

Independent national non-profit. Includes Parents Guide to ADHD in Children

HelpGuide

HelpGuide.org

Resources for mental health and wellness, including ADHD Parenting Tips

appreciations

My deepest thanks go to my wife Judy Sokol for her tireless support, her patience, her enduring faith in me, and her help with many phases of this project. I also have deep gratitude to Rebecca Herskovitz for her help with planning the format of the book as well as with its artistic design.

Numerous friends, family members, and colleagues, including Barbara Weinberg, Patricia Papernow, Abigail Hillman, Paul Neustadt, Ephraim McDowell, Oliver Harper, Art Mones, Nathan Sokol-Margolis and others helped support, critique, and encourage me.

I especially want to thank Shel Horowitz of FrugalMarketing.com for being such a skillful, resourceful, and positive guide throughout the publishing process.

Kathi Dunn and Hobie Hobart of Dunn+Associates Design have patiently and masterfully created a visually arresting and engaging work. I am so grateful to them for their support and expertise.

And, thanks to Sarah Lynne Reul, the illustrator of this book, for her creative and skillful depictions of the characters, as well as her patience and sensitivity in our work together.

About the Author

Barton S. Herskovitz, MD, is a board-certified psychiatrist who practices in Newton and Needham, Massachusetts. For more than thirty years, he has specialized in helping families of ADHD and oppositional children. He's run many groups for parents of children with ADHD, for children, teens, and adults who have ADHD, as well as workshops for siblings.

A former instructor at Harvard Medical School, he has conducted research on ADHD in families, given numerous talks on the subject, and written about the challenges faced by siblings of ADHD kids. He lives in Cambridge, Massachusetts.

Dr. Herskovitz can be reached at www.ADHDSiblingChallenge.com/contact.

About the Illustrator

Sarah Lynne Reul is an illustrator and an award-winning 2D animator, who has written and illustrated several children's books. Her work can be found at www.Reuler.com.

Made in the USA
Monee, IL
22 March 2021